The Search for

by Ele
Illustrated by Emma Levey

OXFORD

UNIVERSITY PRESS

In this story …

Pip and Kit run *Finders Squeakers* – a lost and found agency. They help return lost things to their owners.

Chapter 1
Pack your warm clothes!

Pip and Kit were in the den, working on Pip's latest invention: a new <u>style</u> of aeroplane powered by solar energy. Just as they finished, the screen behind them started flashing. Someone needed their help!

Pip has invented a new <u>style</u> of aeroplane. Can you imagine how it might be different from a normal <u>style</u> of aeroplane?

An image of a fluffy grey penguin appeared on the screen.

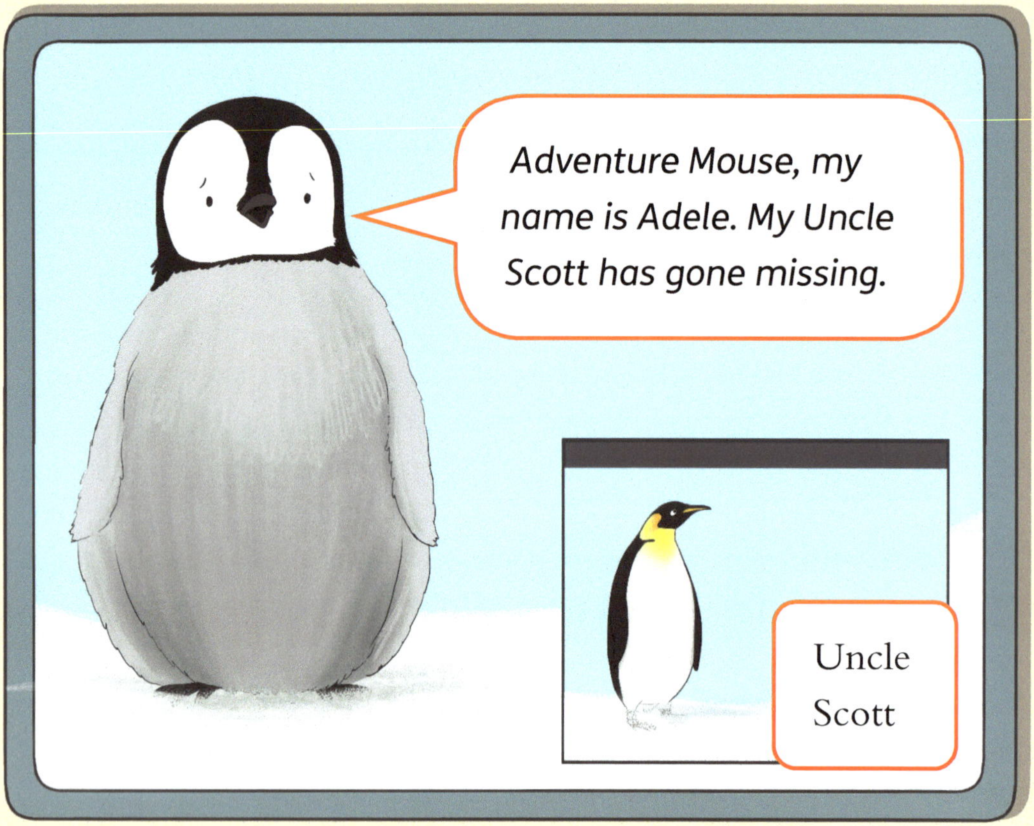

> Adventure Mouse, my name is Adele. My Uncle Scott has gone missing.

Uncle Scott

Pip typed a <u>response</u>. *Where was he last seen?*
Adele replied: *Antarctica.*
Pip turned to Kit. "Pack your warm clothes!" she said. "We've got a penguin to find!"

What other questions could Pip have asked in <u>response</u> to Adele's message?

It was the perfect opportunity to test the new plane.

"Will it make it all the way to Antarctica?" Kit asked, loading their packs.

"Of course!" Pip replied. "At least, I hope so."

Pip and Kit pushed the plane out of the den and jumped into the cockpit. Then, whirring and spluttering, the plane took off.

They whizzed over land and sea.

After many hours, they saw the ice of Antarctica below them. The little plane began to shake.

"The solar battery's running low!" yelled Pip. She steered the plane down. "Hold on! It's going to be a bumpy landing!"

The plane thumped down and skidded into a huge snowdrift.

Pip and Kit jumped out of the plane, landing with a crunch in the snow.

A penguin waddled quickly over to meet them. It was Adele. She looked miserable. "We've looked and looked, but we can't find Uncle Scott anywhere!"

Can you show Adele's miserable expression? Can you show the opposite of a miserable expression?

"Uncle Scott wants to be an explorer," Adele explained, "but he has a terrible sense of direction. What if he's lost?"

"Don't worry," Pip said, trying to sound confident. "We'll find your uncle and bring him back safely."

"Watch out for orcas," Adele said.

Kit gulped and clutched his compass.

Pip pulled her scarf tighter. "Right, let's go!" she said.

Together, Pip and Kit set off to search for the missing penguin.

Chapter 2
The heat sensor

"Antarctica is huge," Kit said, his teeth chattering. "How are we going to find Scott?"

Pip removed her backpack. Then she pulled out a shiny object. "I brought a heat sensor," she said. "Scott's body is warmer than the ice. This sensor can detect his heat and show us where he is."

Pip removed her backpack. Does this mean that she put it on or took it off? What might you remove when you go indoors after being outside?

The sensor showed a mix of reds, yellows and greens as Pip pointed it at Kit. It showed dark blue when she pointed it at the ice.

"Look! What's that?" Pip gasped.

On the sensor, something glowed in the distance … and it was moving.

Pip and Kit raced towards it.

As they got closer, the shape on the screen grew larger … and larger … and larger.

"Pip," Kit said, in a worried voice, "I don't think that's a penguin."

Just then, an enormous orca surged up from a hole in the ice.

"Run!" Pip yelled.

The orca splashed back down into the icy water. A huge, freezing-cold wave whooshed up into the air.

"Take cover!" Kit called.

They both dived beneath an ice ledge. The freezing-cold water rained down all around, but Pip and Kit stayed dry.

"I think I'll adjust the heat sensor to look for something more penguin-sized," Pip said.

Pip and Kit hurried on. The wind picked up, making them both shiver.

Soon, Pip saw something that made her heart leap. It was a patch of heat, about the size that a penguin might produce.

To produce something means to make it. Pip sees a shape that is producing heat. Do you think you produce more heat when you're sitting still or when you're moving around?

"This way!" Pip cried. "It might be Scott."

It wasn't long before they saw a black-and-white shape, huddled all alone on the ice sheet.

"Scott!" Kit called.

Scott looked up, waved a wing and waddled over to meet them.

"Adele sent us," Pip explained. "She's been so worried. Are you all right?"

Scott nodded sadly. "I'm sorry to be such a bother," he said. "I wanted to be the first penguin to trek right across Antarctica. Then I got lost."

"Well, we've found you," Kit said. He held up his compass. "I've been keeping track of our direction. This will help us find the way back to your home."

"I don't know how to thank you," Scott said.

"Don't thank us just yet," Pip replied. "We're not out of trouble. It looks like there's a storm on its way."

Scott and Kit followed Pip's gaze. Dark-grey clouds hid the sun. Snowflakes swirled in the wind.

17

"We have to get back," Scott warned. "We don't want to get caught in a snowstorm."

Kit held out his compass. The needle swung and pointed north. Kit turned the compass and found the right direction. "This way," he said, striding off. "We should be back soon."

Chapter 3
Wind-powered penguin

They walked as quickly as they could, crunching over the snow, but the dark clouds were getting closer and closer.

"Hurry!" Pip called. "Run!"

However, it was hard to run in the snow.

"It's no good," Kit cried. "We won't beat the storm on foot!"

"If we can't run, maybe we can slide!" Pip exclaimed. "Kit, can you get your tent and spare flying goggles out?" As Kit unpacked his tent, Pip turned to Scott. "How would you like to be the first wind-powered penguin?" she asked.

A grin spread across Scott's face.

A minute later, Pip had turned the tent into a huge kite.

"Climb aboard!" Scott cried, as he flopped on to his belly.

Kit held on to the ropes. A gust of wind blew into the kite, lifting it into the air. Scott shot across the ice.

"Whee!" Kit yelled. "This is what I call travelling in style!"

"Look out!" Pip warned. "There's a crevasse!"
There was a huge crack in the ice up ahead.
"Hold on!" Kit shouted. He pulled on one of the ropes and they swerved towards a ramp of ice.
They shot up the ice ramp, lifted off the ground and sailed over the crevasse!

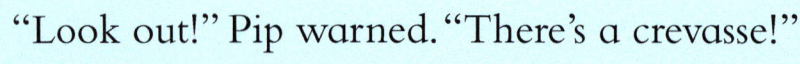

"Over there!" Pip called.

Rows and rows of penguins stood watching the storm clouds in the sky.

Scott skidded to a halt.

Adele rushed forward to greet them. "Uncle Scott!" she cried. "You're safe."

Scott hugged Adele.

"I'm glad you made it back before the storm hits," said Adele.

Just then, thick snowflakes started to fall and settle on Kit's nose.

"We need to get under cover," Pip said.

"I have a better idea!" Scott replied.

Chapter 4
Safe in the huddle

The penguins started to gather around Pip and Kit. They huddled close together.

"We'll keep you warm," Adele said.

Pip and Kit were snuggled in the centre of the penguins, cosy among all of the feathers.

The storm struck. The wind howled above their heads. Snow whirled around them.

However, in the huddle, Pip, Kit and the penguins stayed warm and safe.

"I can't believe we're in the middle of a snowstorm," Pip said to Kit. "I feel as warm as toast!"

When the storm was finally over, the huddle broke apart.

"See?" Adele said to Scott. "It's best for penguins to stick together."

Scott sighed. "I know I shouldn't have wandered off by myself, but I really wanted to be an explorer."

"I have an idea," Adele said to Scott. "Next time you go exploring, you should take a team, and I can come with you!"

"That's a wonderful idea," Scott said.

"Here, this might come in handy, too," Kit added. He took his compass off and hung it around Scott's neck.

Whee!

"Thank you," Scott said to Pip and Kit. "How can I ever repay you?"

Pip looked at their plane, which was still stuck in the snowdrift. "Could you help dig us out?" she asked.

Scott laughed. "We'll get rid of that snow in no time."

The penguins all worked together, and soon the plane was free.

How would you get rid of all the snow from the plane? What might you use?

Pip checked the battery. "Fully charged!" she said. "Luckily there was enough sun to charge it before the storm."

Pip and Kit climbed back into the plane and waved goodbye to Adele, Scott and the other penguins.

Then they took off across the ice.

As they flew home, Pip thought about the warm huddle. She remembered the teamwork that kept the penguins safe.

"Everyone needs friends," she said, "even explorers."

"Even detectives," Kit replied. "I'm glad we have each other."

"I couldn't agree more," Pip replied.

Read and discuss

Read and talk about the following questions.

Page 3: If you had a plane, would it be in a solar-powered style like Kit and Pip's, or in a different style? Why?

Page 4: If someone asked you what the best part of this story was, what would your response be?

Page 7: How do you think Pip and Kit felt when they saw Adele's miserable expression?

Page 10: Can you describe some things that you remove from your bag at school every day?

Page 14: Can you talk about something that you have produced in an art lesson at school?

Page 29: When might someone say: "Can you get rid of that, please?"